C000144153

RESCUED

By Andy L. Vistrand

The HillHelen Group Publishers LLC

Copyright ©2023 by Andy L. Vistrand.

All rights reserved. No part of this book may be reproduced or utilized in any form or by any means, electronic or mechanical, including photocopy, recording, or by an information storage and retrieval system, without permission in writing from the publisher.

Library of Congress Control Number: 2023920382

ISBN: 979-8-9873201-9-8

Printed and bound in the United States of America
by Ingram Lightning Source.

First Edition

Editors: Jacque Hillman, Kim Stewart
Layout and design: Kim Stewart
Cover painting by artist and illustrator
Wanda Stanfill of Jackson, Tennessee

The HillHelen Group LLC
470 North Pkwy. Suite C
Jackson, TN 38305

The HillHelen Group LLC
635 North 65th Place
Mesa, AZ 85205

(731) 394-2894
www.hillhelengrouppublishers.com
hillhelengroup@gmail.com

Praise for *Rescued* and Andy L. Vistrand

My first encounter with Andy was in an interview for a police officer job position in 2013. Right away his drive, team commitment, and patriotism caught my attention.

Whether it was his solid raising, the Corps or a mixture, you could tell he was designed and molded to serve people. In his law enforcement days he wore the uniform with pride; he concentrated heavily on performing his duties to a high standard. His dedication and conscientious performance stood out. A straight shooter no matter the consequences, Andy is willing to stand for what is right no matter the cost. His writings should take us on awesome journey!

—Jeff McCoy

I first met Andy at the Nashville, Tennessee, Police Academy. There was something about him that felt like he had been my best friend since childhood. Andy was the most intense individual, but the funniest guy ever.

Andy also has another quality about him that I admire: his patriotism. One day, near the end of our training, one of the instructors came in screaming about how the halyard had worked loose from the cleat, and the national flag was on the ground.

Andy was in charge of the detail that raised and lowered the flag every day. I saw Andy's face when he heard the instructor, and you would have thought Andy let down every person in America. He ran out to the flag pole and corrected his mistake along with his detail. The instructors liked to inflict pain on us, so he ordered Andy to run "The Hill" until he puked. Andy did as he was told, but also felt he deserved the punishment. When I looked outside, I saw Andy running to his punishment site, but his detail was right behind him. They all took the punishment together. If we could all be as patriotic and intense as Andy, our country would be unstoppable.

—Scott Whitmire

Funny story. I met Andy when he started working for the Trenton Police Department, and I was the assistant public defender who handled that court in 2013. Initially, Andy would not even speak to me.

As someone who has put his life on the line for my freedom—and as someone who has pinned on a badge, kissed his wife and children goodbye, then walked out the door to go to work not knowing if he would make it home—Andy believed I was the bad guy. I respect that. Once Andy got to know me, we have become what I hope will be lifelong friends!

When Andy told me he was writing a book, I just knew he and the book would be successful. I am in awe of Andy's whatever-it-takes attitude. His honor, valor, and pride show through in all he does. To Andy, giving 110 percent to all he undertakes is more than duty. It is who he is. Expect a second-to-none reading experience!

—Milly Worley

On October 13, 2013, I was lining into a formation about to endeavor into the Police Academy. While pushing the earth's crust into itself, I heard a sound behind me.

Looking back, I saw the face of a man who was focused, determined, and confident. This man, later to be my roommate, was none other than Andy Vistrand. This man was hard-working, business-driven, goal-oriented, and best of all, loyal to his family.

As we progressed through the academy and our police career, our families become increasingly involved. I later left law enforcement to pursue a self-employment opportunity and the majority of the blue family fell off. Not Andy, nor his family. He is the absolute definition of integrity, and I couldn't be more honored to be a part of his life. This book will have his heart and soul poured throughout it as everything else he conquers. Thank you for holding my six.

—Clint Warrington

I've had the pleasure of knowing Andy for twelve years, having met through the Marine Corps League. If I had to use one word to describe Andy, it would be passionate. Anything he endeavors is pursued with 100 percent effort.

Lots of people think about writing a book, few follow through. Andy is a man of action. Expect nothing less than an exceptional reading experience!

—**Thomas Montgomery**

After almost twenty years of knowing Andy, I can say confidently that he is an equal mix of integrity, resilience, and authenticity. Never afraid to face a challenge and always eager to pursue his passions, you are in store for a great read in this and all future works by my friend and author, Andy Vistrand!

—**Major Ronald Chino, USMC Retired**

Marine Corps veteran Andy L. Vistrand created a book promotion prop that became a kind of keepsake, honoring the dog that saved him and commemorating his first book published.

PREFACE

This is a story of how a hardened combat veteran found peace with an unexpected canine companion. Our meeting was surely influenced by a higher power; there is no other way to explain the circumstances that brought us together.

I was in no position to care for an animal. I could barely care for myself at the time.

The relationship blossomed from one of necessity to one of pure love, commitment, personal and professional growth, and understanding. We were blessed with Dozer. He provided us with the purest form of love that only a dog could provide. He was our family, and we were his.

Dozer's existence and inclusion in this family was as genuine as any human being could have been. His absence has been painful, and his presence has been sorely missed. This family will endure and move on, but we will always remember Dozer.

I chose to compose this literary piece to document our lives with Dozer and pay respects to him. He gave us far more than we could have asked for, and I want to share our journey. I also want to make people aware that a dog can really make a positive and meaningful impact on our lives.

Acknowledgments

John and Donna Vistrand for allowing me to proofread my work with you.

Jamie Vistrand for proofreading my work.

Scott Vistrand for proofreading my work.

Jamie, Xander, Brantley, Bailey, and Skip Vistrand for allowing me to pursue this venture, and for supporting me.

Chaplain Keith Guinn for the assistance with scripture.

Thomas Montgomery for putting me in touch with people who got me started on my journey to become an author.

Dennis Renshaw and Frank McMeen for speaking with me about becoming an author.

The many professionals who provided character testimonials for me.

Photographer Becky Stafford for professional head shots.

And last but not least, Jacque Hillman, her team, and the editorial board of The HillHelen Group LLC for allowing my dream to be realized.

Table of Contents

Andy L. Vistrand's dog, Dozer, was more than a best friend. He was family.

"I found myself in some
dark and unprecedented times . . .
My life would soon change."

INTRODUCTION

"He is the one you praise; He is your God, who performed for you those great and awesome wonders you saw with your own eyes."

Deuteronomy 10:21

Faith and a Fated Friendship

Our faith is one of the most closely guarded subject matters in life. Next to political stance, religious beliefs are not something we share with just anyone. Defining faith is nearly impossible, as it means something different for each person.[1]

We've all heard that God works in mysterious ways. God works magic as only he can and makes the impossible a reality. Our God is an awesome God. He gives each of us what we need. That may be support, luck, protection, or hope offered in our darkest hours. Sometimes things do not go the way we anticipate; those moments can be difficult to process.

Even in our most dire moments, we must keep the faith. It's a fact of life—things do not always go the way we want or expect them to. Many times when this has happened to me, the next opportunity to come along is much better than the first.

Faith in a higher power helps us summon that inner strength to endure, or to take action if that is necessary. There are no answers for the miracles to which he guides us. He always has a plan for us, and there are times that our desires and his intentions do not jive. Accepting this fact may be hard. Little did I know, I would soon get a front-row seat to this lesson.

Owning a dog may seem like a chore to some, but for most people it is more reward than work. The relationship between human beings and canines has been evolving for the last 15,000 to 40,000 years. The vast number of benefits a dog provides is interesting. Dogs are so much more than simple companions. Owning a dog has been shown to reduce anxiety, stress, and illness. Dogs have been linked to improved mood and increased energy of up to ten hours after interaction.[2]

A study of 975 dog owners showed that dogs rank closely to spouses or romantic partners, and higher than friends, children, parents, and siblings when owners were asked to whom they turn when feeling a variety of ways.[3]

Canine interaction has proven so widely effective that many college campuses and hospitals allow visits from furry four-legged friends. In fact, dog interaction has helped some hospital patients cut back on pain medications. The health benefits do not stop there. Life with dogs can reduce the risk of contracting a cardiovascular disease. Of those who have already suffered from a cardiac event, such as heart attack, it was concluded that non-dog owning survivors were found to be four times more likely to become deceased in the first year following the cardiac event.[4]

Dogs also help us communicate, sometimes by becoming a conversation starter themselves. Even more fascinating, studies conducted with individuals suffering from intellectual disabilities have experienced increased physical reactions, such as smiling, by up to 30 percent! Interaction with dogs has increased social skills and decreased loneliness in individuals who use a wheelchair.[5]

Researchers also have found that having a dog in your picture on dating platforms leads to more interaction; it makes you seem more approachable and likable. Arguably, owning a dog increases your social status.

The benefits of owning a dog far outweigh the costs. All things considered, it's no wonder people become so emotionally attached to their dogs.

Ignorantly, I had never given the idea of a therapy dog much credibility. I felt like having a therapy dog was an excuse to cling to something for nothing more than attention. Clearly, I am now aware of just how wrong I was.

After separating from the active-duty Marines, I found it difficult to adapt to civilian life. There was no accountability in the civilian sector. There was no discipline in the civilian sector. There were only excuses, and no shortage of those.

Life was difficult. I had lost my identity as an elite warrior, a Marine.

I was used to handling the toughest tasks—including making safe-for-flight determinations for two separate aviation platforms, the AH-1W Super Cobra tandem seat attack helicopter and the UH-1N Huey utility helicopter.

I went from being an integral part of a flight crew for combat missions to just another face in the crowd. The transition took its toll on my personal and professional well-being.

I found myself in some dark and unprecedented times.

I had no idea that the only dose of medicine capable of pulling me out of this nosedive was a dog. My life would soon change, and my viewpoint about therapy dogs would be turned upside down.

Lance Cpl. Andy L. Vistrand, a UH-1N Huey crew chief assigned to Marine Light/Attack Helicopter Squadron 269, scans the ground to find a target while practicing aerial gunnery. Vistrand fired the .50 caliber machine gun every time he flew, in order to improve his accuracy and ensure the weapon functioned properly. Photo from the US Marine Corps.

CHAPTER 1

"When I am afraid, I put my trust in you.
In God, whose word I praise—in God I trust and am not afraid."

Psalm 56

The Beginning

I was a western New York native, trying to find myself south of the Mason Dixon line. I was a doggone Yankee and worse, in some cases. Natives had a habit of referring to visitors or tourists as Yankees. I earned the "doggone and worse" because unlike most travelers, I stayed in the South.

At age twenty-three, I separated from the active-duty Marine Corps and relocated to Jackson, Tennessee, to begin my new career as a freight conductor aboard trains on CSX Transportation's Memphis Subdivision.

After I completed three tours overseas, *transition* seems like a mild way to describe my adjustment to life in Tennessee.

I went through many dramatic and life-changing moments in Iraq. One of the most vivid occurred on May 2, 2005, when small arms fire shot down our aircraft.

I could hear the bullets whizzing through the rotor arc. By the number of rounds, I fully expected to see a gaping hole in the tail boom. Much to my surprise, there was no evidence to suggest we had even taken damage. After the dust settled, I would later learn that a bullet missed hitting me by four feet or less. Our crew watched as our lead aircraft took multiple rounds. Tracers were going right through the Cobra.

Our captain came over the radio to build our situational awareness, and the message sent chills up my spine.

"Airbursts, airbursts! There are multiple projectiles airborne!"

We sought to break contact immediately. I was given the command to open fire, but on what? I had no identifiable targets.

The pilot's emergency checklist called for us to land immediately after losing transmission oil pressure. We managed to limp the aircraft from the direct line of fire to the open desert, while the upper planetary gears ate themselves to shreds.

It was only a matter of time before we lost the main rotor due to loss of lubrication.

We safely landed the aircraft, pointing the nose toward the likely avenue of enemy approach so that we could bring the crew-served guns to bear, should it be necessary. We spent between three or four hours out in the open desert just south of Husaybah. I was in the prone on an M240G belt-fed machine gun protecting my aircraft and crew with a weapons-free declaration from the pilot in command.

Stacked in the overhead were a pair of AH-1W Super Cobras and a pair of F15 Eagles, which I believe were dispatched to neutralize the aircraft in the event we became overrun and had to abandon our aircraft.

Eventually, we were accompanied by a pair of M1 Abrams main battle tanks on our flanks and an amphibious assault vehicle was bringing more mechanics to our location.

The next day, in an act of defiance, our squadron call sign went

Lance Cpl. Andy L. Vistrand, right, works on a weapon with Cpl. Kyle Lundquist of Brookfield, Connecticut, in August 2005. Vistrand fired a .50 caliber machine gun every time he flew, in order to keep his skills sharp and to keep the weapon working properly. Photo from the US Marine Corps.

from Misfit to Revenge. That moment stuck with me and has ever since. I will probably take it with me to the grave.

I served my country for five years, from 2003 to 2008, and completed three back-to-back tours overseas in 2005, 2006, and 2007. I considered re-enlisting, but thought the grass might be greener on the other side.

Near the end of my contract, I took a Seps/Taps class meant to reintegrate military veterans into civilian life. On June 3, 2008, I departed Marine Corps Air Station New River on terminal leave.

I had no career plans, which is highly unlike me. I filled that gap when I attended a job fair during Seps/Taps class. There were recruiters from many Fortune 500 companies, including CSX Transportation. As a huge rail fan, I immediately set my mind on a new career as a crew member aboard freight trains.

I saw this as a dream job. I jumped at the opportunity, driving eight hundred miles one way to Jackson and staying in a hotel overnight to secure my dream of riding on locomotives and pulling the pins on freight cars. I began my job with CSX Transportation on August 17, 2008.

This was the same date that I officially separated from the active-duty military on paper. Anyone who knows anything about the military or the railroad knows how big of a coincidence this is. No one can plan anything around either of these professions, as both are 24/7/365 operations. They almost always run on a need-to-know basis where circumstances change at a moment's notice. A Marine officer had warned me that life on the railroad was interesting—that it was a feast-and-famine lifestyle and that I could expect to be laid off at some point in my career. He was absolutely right.

Some days, there was too much work and not enough people to do it. Others, there was too little work and too many people. The railroad is such a variable job, highly influenced by the economy.

On January 28, 2009, I received the call from an automated source advising me that I had been "displaced," which was another way of telling me I was being furloughed.

I felt like I had the rug ripped out from underneath me. The situation challenged my resilience.

In crept the first fear I had in re-inventing myself. This may have been my first realization that I was in a seemingly hopeless situation and in need of being rescued.

How was it that a combat-hardened Marine was being reduced from personal and professional greatness, to that of a lone, misplaced soul lost in a deep sea of average Joes? I was trying to put my life together and prove to the world that there was life after being an elite American warrior.

By a stroke of luck, I was called back to work for a short two-week stint due to some vandal burning a bridge down on another

Lance Cpl. Andy L. Vistrand conducts a cockpit check as part of daily and turnaround inspections on a UH-1N Huey. Photo from the US Marine Corps.

CSX subdivision in Alabama. This circumstance increased the opportunity to catch work, as there would be a host of re-routed freight trains coming across my home rail territory, the Memphis subdivision.

I was able to mark up and work an assignment train, Q528, that was expected to be annulled shortly. Annulled is railroad jargon for terminated. Knowing the fate of the assignment, the regular conductor who held that job fled to the extra board to work over the road. The assignment was exactly as advertised: short-lived. I worked maybe two weeks, and I was laid off again with no idea how long it might last.

The year 2009 was a tough one. I was unemployed for the first time in my life. I had nothing but time to sit and ponder the many ways I had gone wrong after active-duty separation. I was living on an extremely limited income, and my personal motivation and confidence had taken a beating.

I had met the woman who would later become my wife, though I didn't know that at the time. But I was ashamed of where I was, personally and professionally. I could not imagine what she saw in me. I felt like it was a matter of time before she would be gone, like my dream job.

I was hopeless, and so was the job market.

When I separated from the Marines, I entered an economy plagued by the Great Recession. After the housing bubble burst, the national average unemployment rate reached its peak in October 2009 at 10 percent.[6]

I was collateral damage.

I endured the agony of unemployment for nearly a year and a half, always wondering when the phone might ring and the railroad would call me back to duty.

It was an empty hope. My run with the railroad would end in resignation in July 2010, after a lot of unrewarded patience and frustration. The next month, I started a new career as a team leader with Carlisle Engineered Transportation Solutions, manufacturing tread to be used in building tires for all-terrain, agricultural, construction vehicles, and trailers.

Before I finally landed that job, I thought about moving back home but couldn't live with the idea of accepting defeat.

After all, I had survived three combat tours in Iraq, and the indomitable fighting spirit, commonplace in all Marines, would not allow me to count this as a loss. I was doing what Marines do best, making the best of the worst. I hoped something positive would come of it, even if that meant taking the proverbial bull by the horns and manipulating the situation, if possible.

Then came Dozer.

Someone abandoned a puppy at my apartment complex.

I do not have any idea how people can be so cruel. If I could, at the very least, I would have a conversation with the individual who did this. Perhaps much more than that. However, I cannot be too mad. That person's loss was truly my gain.

A neighbor had bathed the puppy. The teenagers next door wanted to keep it, but their parents did not allow that. Another missed opportunity for the puppy would again redirect the trajectory of a meeting. A divine power was assuredly confirming the meet that would soon happen.

This photo from 2009 shows little Dozer as a puppy, not long after Andy L. Vistrand found him loitering around his apartment complex in Jackson.

CHAPTER 2

"Two are better than one, because they have a good return for their labor: If either of them falls down, one can help the other up. But pity anyone who falls and has no one to help them up. Also, if two lie down together, they will keep warm. But how can one keep warm alone? Though one may be overpowered, two can defend themselves."

Ecclesiastes 4:9-12

The Meet

December 15, 2009. I was in no hurry. I waited until around 9 p.m. to go get my mail to avoid human contact. I left my apartment and turned right to descend the stairwell to the sidewalk.

At the bottom of the stairs, a small brown puppy stared up at me. He was very friendly and followed me to the office building, which housed the mailboxes for the entire complex. After I collected my mail, he trailed me back across the parking lot. I returned to my apartment with puppy in tow.

It was mid-December in the South. Although it never got as cold as it had in my native New York State, I could not leave

Dozer's playful antics in the snow inspired his name.

him outside. I let him in, and he immediately found his way to my master bedroom, where he fell fast asleep under the skirt of my queen-sized bed. I called my girlfriend and told her that I had a puppy in my possession, which surprised her. After her shift was over, she came home from Somerville to bring a kennel.

The dog was a handsome, mixed-breed puppy. He had brown eyes, was predominantly brown in color, and had a little white blotch on his chest. He seemed to be in good health, other than having fleas.

Still, I had no intention of becoming a pet owner. *If I can't care for myself, I can't care for an animal,* I thought. This was me being brutally honest with myself and taking the high road as a responsible person. I was down to the last edible resources in my apartment—an opened box of Honey Nut Cheerios, which I was now sharing with the dog.

In the days that followed, there were many serious conversations regarding the dog's status.

I talked to my girlfriend, and I shared my fears.

"If you don't adopt him, I will," she replied.

That was all the motivation I needed.

Our family was just beginning, and this helpless pup would be part of it right from the start.

It seemed like there never was a dog who loved snow more than Dozer. He got his name for the way he played in snow—bulldozing it around with his chest and legs. His new family loved to watch him enjoy the winter weather.

CHAPTER 3

*"All this, I have in writing as a result of the Lord's hand on me,
and he enabled me to understand all the details of the plan."*

1 Chronicles 28:19

The Details

We considered many names, but we finally agreed to call him
Dozer because of a peculiar habit. He would place his chest
on the ground and push snow around with his front legs. It was
a sight to behold. I have never seen a dog so excited about snow.

Dozer had medium-length hair and really enjoyed the cold
weather. I used to jokingly refer to him as a sled dog, because of his
joy in the frigid temperatures. Jamie and I took him out to play in
the snow any chance we got. He enjoyed catching snowballs.

We took him to the vet as soon as possible. He was treated
for fleas, dewormed, vaccinated, neutered, and microchipped. His
rabies tag was prominently displayed on his harness.

Dozer was a good puppy. Eventually, I trained him to sit and
lie down. Additionally, he learned *Semper fi* and *freeze. Semper fi,*
Latin for "always faithful," is a Marine motto. For Dozer, it was the

command to raise his right foot in the air above his right eyebrow. It looked like a salute, or at least the best salute a dog could give considering his circumstances. Upon the command *freeze*, Dozer would sit up on his rear haunches and raise both front legs in the air as if he were being stopped by police.

Dozer was an easygoing, lovable dog. He was always there to raise your spirits, no matter how hard or bad things were for you. He was mild-mannered, and rarely barked or created a ruckus. Dozer was also anxious, which no doubt had something to do with how he was abandoned in an apartment complex so early in life.

Dozer's actual birthdate was unknown to anyone but him. We chose to celebrate his birthday on October 7 every year, as this was the approximate date that we calculated based on the veterinarian's

assessment of his age. Dozer's first birthday was a big deal. Jamie and I had moved out of our individual apartments, and we were now living together in a townhouse. We invited seven guests for his party—Jamie's father, her best friend, and her family.

We went all out, with pup-cakes, gifts, and cards for the birthday boy. I'm sure some thought we were crazy, going on and on about this dog, but he was our family and the closest thing we had to a child. Full-grown, Dozer typically weighed around thirty-seven to forty pounds. He did have a moment in time where he got to be as heavy as sixty pounds. I took him to the vet. His diet had not changed, but he was gaining weight quickly.

Blood work showed he suffered from hypothyroidism. His weight gain caused him to become lethargic and reclusive, often lying in his bed and avoiding human contact. This was also very uncharacteristic of him, as he enjoyed our family and was always close by when we gathered in the living room. Dozer responded well to treatment with a prescription drug which he was given every morning with peanut butter. Eventually, he returned to his original weight and was much more social.

One day we decided to take Dozer to Chickasaw State Park for a little relaxing walk. What was supposed to be a day of leisure soon turned into anguish, as we made a critical error in judgment.

Dozer at Chickasaw State Park.

We thought maybe we could trust Dozer off the leash. We took him off the leash and allowed him to walk freely with us. In theory, this was the ideal setup. In reality, nothing went according to plan. He bolted, and we were scared half to death we would never get him back. He would not come to us when called. He became more frightened the closer I got to him. He was impossible to catch.

If not for a dirt bike rider who helped us secure Dozer, we would have never got our dog back. From that day forward, he never came off the leash again.

I could always tell when Dozer felt good. He would often drop his left front shoulder, burying it in the carpet and curl his head around as if he was looking at his own tail. He did that when he was happy and wanted his hips rubbed. I would always oblige and even came up with a name for the awkward position, the tripod. As silly as it sounds, I was always happy to see him do this. Something about that playful spirit did something for my heart and soul. It comforted me to know that life, no matter how bad at one point, can get better. I was happy that he was happy with me and my family. This was one of the many reasons I loved Dozer and why my life would be incomplete without a dog like him.

Dozer was the needed distraction that pulled me from my own headspace. His innocence and vigor for life kept me going. This dog gave me a new focus and sense of purpose. His life could have been tragic, as mine could have been. Together, we were able to move on and rewrite the script.

My wife, whom I was dating while this whole scenario played out, will tell you that she noticed a change in my moods and behavior during those difficult days. She attributed it to the fact that I now had something to do with my time.

He definitely kept me busy. The thing I loved most about Dozer was his ability to talk to me without speaking a word. One of the best non-verbal ways for him to communicate with me was when he would come up to me after dinner while I was still sitting at the table and nudge my arm while laying his head flat on my leg. It was as if he were telling me, "Okay, Dad, you have eaten, now it's my turn. Please feed me."

It was a sweet gesture and illustrated the depth of his love and trust in me. He did this often later on in life, and it reinforced for me how solid we were together. The dog we have now does not do this, and I miss this interaction. I realize that every animal has its own personality, but this is one of the things I miss so dearly about my Dozer.

CHAPTER 4

"Your eyes will see strange sights,
and your mind will imagine confusing things."
Proverbs 23:33

The Peculiar

As strange as it sounds, Dozer loved plastic water bottles. No one could place a plastic bottle on the coffee table without him sitting there barking at it or attempting to shove the bottle over with his nose. He would beg, whine, moan, and have a fit, until he received the bottle. Then he would proceed to chew off the bottle cap. He enjoyed the crunchy sides while chewing on the slightly deflated bottle.

About chewing—all puppies love to chew. I distinctly remember a time when I fully expected that his chewing would land both of us in the doghouse, or worse.

One day while on my computer, I heard some wood snap or break downstairs. Creeping down the stairs, I went into the living room to investigate the noise. I sneaked through the living room, and into the passageway to the dining room. That is when I saw it.

Andy L. Vistrand's dog, Dozer, had a lot of great qualities for a sidekick. His chewing habit was not one of them.

I was horrified.

Dozer had developed a taste for wood. Much like a beaver, he had nearly chewed straight through the center of the rear rung supporting the legs of Jamie's expensive dining room chair. I was so shocked I literally felt the color leave my face, and I was instantaneously paralyzed with fear.

How could I tell Jamie that the dog had snacked on her expensive Henco formal dining room chair?

She had told me she regretted not picking up more chairs when she bought the set, and now this one was likely doomed. It really looked like a beaver had assaulted the chair. There were scraps of wood littering the floor beneath it.

"No! You didn't!" I said, grabbing my head in pure panic.

In my mind, there was no way this was going to be okay.

Dozer had Andy L. Vistrand's girlfriend, Jamie, charmed from the start. Neither he nor Andy were in the doghouse for long after Dozer's chewing habit got him into trouble.

Even if I had survived the great economic recession, there was no way I would survive this—and if for some reason I did, the relationship was surely over.

Luckily for me and the dog, Jamie is a very understanding person. She forgave us both, and my dad, Jamie, and I repaired the chair together. It turned out so well that you couldn't tell it had been damaged unless you knew the whole story. I am still relieved this one worked out.

Coincidentally, years later we would sell that nice, lightly used table-and-chair set the day that Dozer passed away.

It seemed like a sign from heaven that Dozer had arrived, and he was trying to make us smile about something. It was another uncanny experience that only God could have influenced.

Channeling his inner beaver wasn't Dozer's only bad habit.

He had another peculiar trait that was fairly off-putting. When he was scared or startled, he would emit this foul odor—pungent, persistent, and annoying. I jokingly referred to the smell as *Eau de Caca*, for obvious reasons.

And that wasn't the only new phrase he inspired.

As I aged, my hair began to thin, especially on top. I assumed it was due to wearing a flight helmet for most of my enlistment, though I am sure showering in Euphrates River water did not help. I would get on the floor with Dozer to love on and play with him. Dozer would affectionately lick my head, as if I were dirty and in need of cleaning. I joked that he was applying my *Do-gaine,* a combination of *Dozer* and *Rogaine.* Much to my dismay, Do-gaine never yielded any results.

CHAPTER 5

*"Now then, please swear to me by the LORD that you will show
kindness to my family, because I have shown kindness to you."*

Joshua 2:12

The Family

Dozer loved everyone in our family. He would sit in the window of our apartment or home and wait until someone returned home from errands or work.

He often appeared to be on patrol, sitting in the large windows of our townhome when we lived in the apartment complex. There were windows on the first and second floors, where he sat and watched, sometimes for hours on end.

Later on, when we moved into our current home, he sat in the bay windows of our master bedroom and waited on my wife, father-in-law, or my parents. Many times, he got so excited to see someone return that he would leave our bedroom with ears laid back, prancing and wagging his tail. He would get so overcome with joy, he would let out a short, happy bark. It was obvious when someone was returning home.

My parents came to town for a visit from our native New York at least once a year, for about a week. It was always good to see them, and Dozer got excited also. Dozer slept in our master bedroom at night. Every morning, Dozer rushed to the other end of the house to the guest bedroom where Mom and Dad stayed. He was eager to check on them. We were amused to see how much he missed them in just six to eight short hours of time.

Mom and Dad always brought snacks for their trip to prevent the need to stop multiple times for food on their 800-mile journey south. Dad always had the knock-off brand cheddar cheese cubes. He ate some on the way down, but a full bag of those cheddar cheese cubes would last well into their visit and may even hold them over for the return trip, or eastbound to visit my brother and his family. Every time the seal on that bag broke, Dozer hastily found his way to the kitchen to beg Dad for a cheese cube. That dog loved cheddar cheese cubes.

My brother, Scott, visited Jamie and me in 2010. That is the first opportunity that he got to meet Dozer, and the first time Dozer met his cousin Zoey, Scott's dog. Zoey and my brother were just as inseparable as Dozer and I were. It was great to watch the two dogs play. They rough-housed until neither of them could stand, and then they would crash on the carpet. Scott and Dozer got along as well as Zoey and I did. Scott once got on the floor with Dozer to play with him. Scott is a pretty big guy. The dog tried to skirt the corner of the coffee table in mid-leap, and while on his knees, Scott snagged him in midair. The dog must have aged five years in that moment. He shed hair like a bomb went off. It was flying through the air in a cloud. Subsequently, an inside joke about the "huge guy" was born.

On July 7, 2011, Jamie and I were to be married. It was a chaotic time. That week, we had bachelor and bachelorette parties, among other things. Jamie had come home from her bachelorette party with a metallic balloon. Filled with helium, it was on the ceiling most of the week but gradually began to descend from the ceiling

Dozer and Zoey, who belonged to Andy L. Vistrand's brother, were fast friends. Their playful antics provided endless amusement for the brothers.

as it lost more and more of its helium. Eventually, the balloon was just low enough to where Dozer could reach the long tether on it. That dog sat there for hours barking and jumping and carrying on.

At times, he got a hold and pulled it down trying to get a bite. It was still too big for him to fit his mouth around, but that did not stop him from trying. That situation kept him entertained for hours. I captured the moment with our newly purchased camcorder, for inclusion in our family home movies.

On March 30, 2013, my brother and his fiancé, Heather, were to be married and our family had traveled to Raleigh, North Carolina, to commemorate the occasion.

One morning prior to the wedding, Dad, Scott, and I worked on strengthening the chairs that encircled the family dining room table by adding some hardware. Scott's home at that time had a pair of sliding glass doors that opened to a small concrete patio.

There was a fence on either side of the property line, but the back property line was wide open, and about thirty-five to forty yards behind the house, there was a tree line.

Dozer sat there looking through the patio doors and appeared to be fixated on something in the woods. We all thought he was seeing things, until we noticed a small herd of deer grazing in the back. They were probably fifteen to twenty yards deep in the woods.

It once was believed that dogs were color blind, thanks to past studies that we now know were inaccurate. More recent research suggests that their perception of color is limited, but dogs are able to see certain hues.[7]

It would have been very difficult for Dozer to see the deer at that distance, with obstructions, but he did!

He sat there watching and following them as they moved through the woods. I still cannot believe how good his eyesight must have been to pick them up. It was everything we could do to pick them out ourselves.

A helium-filled bachelorette party balloon kept Dozer occupied for days.

The Vistrands were never certain about Dozer's breed. Their best guess is Black Mouth Cur, a breed that originated in the American South and became a popular hunting companion. Their coat is typically yellow or light brown. They have drooped ears and a distinct black muzzle. It is thought that the title character in the novel Old Yeller was a Black Mouth Cur. A very active breed, these dogs are known to be wary of strangers but extremely protective of children. The breed is not recognized by the American Kennel Club.[8]

CHAPTER 6

"Listen, I tell you a mystery:
We will not all sleep, but we will all be changed."

1 Corinthians 15:51

The Mystery

We always had a genuine curiosity about Dozer's breed. Our veterinarian had told us that there was a way to identify it by having his DNA tested. This test cost thirty-five dollars. I had always wanted to know, but never enough to pay thirty-five dollars for the test. Best I could tell, he had some Chow in him, but beyond that, I never really knew. One day we took Dozer to PetSmart, as we often did. We did this at least once a year, so he could pick out a toy on his birthday.

As fate would have it, Dozer lifted his leg on an endcap. This was very uncharacteristic of him; he rarely did such heinous things and never in public. I was embarrassed but immediately began cleaning the mess up. Around the corner came another store patron, an older woman, and she was talkative.

"Wow, what a handsome dog! What breed is he?" she asked.

"I have no idea," I replied. "We have been told there is a DNA test that can be performed to identify his breed, but I have never wanted to spend the money."

She told me that he was a Black Mouth Cur. I had never heard of such a thing, but this woman was adamant.

Well, I could not resist. I later Googled Black Mouth Cur. Much to my surprise, a dog strikingly similar to our Dozer was the first image presented. This breed was somewhat of a hunting dog as it was used to hunt bear, raccoon, feral pig, deer, and squirrels, according to Wikipedia.

We finally knew what breed he was! All those years, and all it took was one embarrassing moment of poor judgment on his part and one random stranger to identify our dog!

Some years later, I had a discussion with our veterinarian during a checkup about what breed Dozer was. I told the story of PetSmart, the older woman who schooled me on his breed, and my research afterward.

The vet gave me a blank stare.

"Do you know what a Black Mouth Cur actually is?" she asked.

"No," I said, of course.

"It's a fancy way of saying he is a mutt," she told me.

Just like that, she had killed my buzz. I never felt so stupid.

I was so proud that I had finally cracked the mystery, only to find out it was a more precise way of declaring my dog a mutt.

CHAPTER 7

"Now all has been heard; here is the conclusion of the matter: Fear God and keep his commandments, for this is the duty of all mankind."

Ecclesiastes 12:13

The Duty

Dozer patrolled our property, keeping it free of trespass by anyone, but mostly in the pursuit of squirrels. There are several black walnut trees in the back yard that attract squirrels. As with any dog, but especially with Black Mouth Curs, he loved to chase them. He never caught one. I am not sure he would know what to do if he had, but he always gave it his best try. I made a game out of it. If I saw a squirrel in the back yard, I'd get Dozer all pumped up to cut him loose in pursuit of the rodents.

When the back door came open, he would flatten out—appearing to be six inches off the deck as he shot across the yard. He was a furry missile, locked onto a target.

There were a few times that his interest in unwelcome animals got him into trouble. One night, I could not get him to come into the house. I called and called. In the darkness, it appeared he had something hemmed up on top of our stockade fence.

Finally, I went out to see what was going on. He had an opossum cornered and precariously perched on the fence top, hissing and showing its teeth. Eventually, I managed to call Dozer off.

In June 2020, I was still working from home during the pandemic. I let Dozer out as I had every morning; however, this morning would turn out to be a first for me.

Moments after I had let him out, I heard a scuffle in the stones in our backyard landscaping. I opened the back door to see Dozer in full retreat, sneezing, frothing, and foaming at the mouth. He kept sneezing, and his eyes appeared to be irritated.

I looked on in horror, realizing there could be only one reason for all that: a skunk.

I approached him cautiously, confirming that the skunk had sprayed him.

I left him outside and retreated into our home to advise my wife of the unfortunate event. While I was telling her the horrific story, our three-year-old son, Brantley, let Dozer in the house. He thought he was helping me out. Insert head-smack emoji here!

That day, I worked from home with nearly every window on the first floor open. I took off work at noon, to get some shampoo for Dozer, who had been left out all day. I had placed a water bowl out back for him, and returned home from Petco with anti-skunk shampoo. He was washed no less than ten times that day. I had never seen the dog more miserable. Baths were not his favorite, so it was no easy task to get him cleaned up and deodorized.

Dozer and Brantley, the youngest son of Andy L. and Jamie Vistrand.

Andy L. and Jamie Vistrand with Dozer at their home.

CHAPTER 8

"He made the moon to mark the seasons,
and the sun knows when to go down."

Psalm 104:19

The Changing Seasons

Time went on, and with it, there were visits from family, vacations, day trips to parks, engagement photos, and many other busy moments in life.

My girlfriend, Jamie, and I went from dating and living in separate apartments, to becoming engaged and living in a townhouse. Then we got married and moved into our first, and current, home. From there, we began laying the foundation for our family to grow.

We introduced our first-born, Xander Cole, to the family in March 2014. Dozer was curious about our new baby and checked on him often. We had none of the problems some other new parents with pets experience; it can be quite a transition when introducing a baby to a family pet.

When we brought Xander home, the first several months he

slept in a bassinet next to our master bed. The first times that the baby made a sound, as they tend to do at night, I often heard the dog going to check on him.

Black Mouth Curs are known to be extremely protective of children, sometimes to the point of interfering with parents disciplining their children.[9] Dozer certainly lived up to the breed's love for young people. He was very attentive to our children, and they were very attentive to him.

Dozer took our growing family in stride. In June 2017, we welcomed Brantley Knox to our family ranks, and Dozer continued to impress us with his adaptability.

The boys grew up with Dozer and loved him unconditionally. When they were little, they shared the living room floor with him. There would be plenty of play and wet kisses to go around.

As the boys grew, their love for Dozer grew also. They would all three sprawl out on the living room floor, and they would love on him while watching television or playing Nintendo.

Some of the more fond memories I have of him and the boys are when we would all go out into our back yard and play.

When that dog started running, he would not stop. Many times he would run in figure eights, zipping behind my shed and coming out on the other side. He ran so fast that he would almost be lying over on his side as he shot around the turns. He would run until his tongue dragged.

Like any family dog, Dozer loved being with his people. He enjoyed walking in our subdivision with us too, but you had to go armed with a plastic bag to pick up his mess because that was bound to happen.

Dozer was such a great family dog. All of these memories with him are priceless.

He also was incredibly tolerant by nature. That was a good thing, because children can be rough on a family pet. I should know; I once had a small beagle puppy that lasted for a few days

The Vistrands' sons, Xander and Brantley, grew up with Dozer.

before succumbing to parvo. Prior to that puppy's passing, there is home video of me sitting in the box with him, holding him tightly. It looked like I was choking the ever-loving life out of him.

I was proud of that dog. Ironically, I named him Lucky. Clearly he was anything but, because he did not live long after contracting the disease.

Dozer loved everyone in his family, and his affection was returned in abundance from the Vistrand children, from Andy's brother Scott, and from Andy and Jamie's parents. Dozer was very attentive to the Vistrands' sons, Xander and Brantley.

Dozer riding in the car with Andy L. Vistrand and his family.

"I wanted so badly for there to be
some kind of remedy,
but I was preparing for the worst."

CHAPTER 9

"I went away full,
but the Lord has brought me back empty."

Ruth 1:21

The Tragedy

Dozer had been fighting some health issues since October 2022. He became ill while were away on vacation. My parents, who had moved to a town just ten miles north of us the year before, were caring for him while we were away in Pensacola, Florida.

Dozer showed symptoms of exhaustion and pain; he was unsteady on his feet, and nearly fell down the short flight of stairs at our back door. My parents were deeply concerned, but we had no reason to assume any worse and suspected that his anxiety was getting the best of him. Dozer always had anxiety; we figured it was from having been abandoned in the Bradford Chase housing complex, thirteen years prior. I only wish it could have been something that simple.

When we got home from vacation, I took Dozer to the veterinarian. She examined him from head to toe, took blood samples, and did a fecal exam. She concluded that he was severely anemic and further diagnosed him with pancreatitis. She prescribed medication but told me outright that she was afraid that due to his extreme anemia, there was no way she could rule out some type of invasive cancer.

Of course, I was not happy to hear this, but considering his age, I was not terribly surprised, either. I dreaded where this was going, but remained hopeful that medication could treat this and mend him.

December 17, 2022, was possibly the saddest day of my life.

My wife and I had been dreading Saturday morning because we knew what could be ahead of us.

Earlier that week, we had returned home from the deactivation of my US Marine Helicopter squadron, HMLA 269. The very next day, we had a stressful personal engagement that we attended. On our way home from that, I contacted our veterinarian to see where we stood, and to find out what could be done, if anything, regarding Dozer's health. I wanted so badly for there to be some kind of remedy, but I was preparing for the worst.

I tried to put it out of my head, but as I woke up on Saturday morning, reality began slowly sinking in. I contacted my brother via Facebook messenger, and we let him and my nieces see Dozer for what would be the very last time. It was harder than I had imagined. My parents showed up to say their goodbyes. There wasn't a dry eye in the house. We had no idea how much harder it was going to get.

CHAPTER 10

"I am Alpha and Omega,
the beginning and the end, the first and the last."

Revelation 22:13

The End

We took Dozer for his final walk in the front yard before we left. I loaded him into my wife's vehicle, and we left for the veterinarian's office. I took the last photo of him riding on the floorboard of the Chevrolet Traverse. I lovingly stroked his head all the way, dreading every second of what lay ahead. I looked at him, remembering all the good times we shared, realizing that our time together may be nearing its end. This surreal moment will be forever engrained in my memory.

Dozer meant so much to me and this family. He was about to be taken from us, to be with the Lord. We were making the decision to end his suffering for him, a selfless act of love and respect for an animal that gave us so much joy and happiness. Such a tough and painful decision to make, but we owed it to him. Dozer had given us so much more than could be expected from a family pet. He had given me an outlet to distract myself from the difficult moments that I survived in a post-military setting in 2009. He had been a loyal companion, had loved and played with our family. He loved us unconditionally, and we loved him in the same manner.

My heart was overwhelmingly heavy. In those moments of reflection, the subject took my breath, as if I were having a panic attack. I felt as though I would hyperventilate, and then a flood of emotions, including pain, sorrow, and a lost feeling, crept in, as I wondered how I could go on without him.

I worried and hoped we were strong enough to be able to make the right decision for him, because selfishly, I did not want to say goodbye to Dozer. He had saved my life.

In a social media post, I shared the following:

> This isn't the first time and won't be the last we will deal with something like this. Our family is devastated. We had to make the heart-wrenching decision to put our dog to sleep this morning.
>
> While I know this was the right decision for him due to various health reasons, it has certainly had a significant impact on us. He has been an integral part of our family unit for a little over thirteen years.
>
> To say that this has left a hole in our hearts is simply far too great an understatement. Please bear with me while I try to pay homage to our component of man's best friend.
>
> I take you back to a cold mid-December night in 2009 in Jackson, Tennessee, at the Bradford Chase apartment complex. I was going through some really dark times, having freshly separated from the military and relocated hundreds of miles from where I grew up with the intention of making a new life for myself post active-duty Marines.

The Vistrands cuddle with Dozer for one last family photo.

While on my way to collect the mail that night, I encountered a flea-infested puppy that followed me to the mailroom.

Little did I know that someone had abandoned him at my apartment complex. He was cute and appeared to need a home.

I was sympathetic to the fact that it was cold and allowed him to come into my apartment to warm up. The dog entered my home and immediately retired to my master bedroom, where he fell fast asleep under the skirt of my bed. The dog that found his way into my apartment that night never left my home, or our hearts, and later became known to us as Dozer.

At the time, I was laid off from employment with the railroad, CSX Transportation, and could barely afford to take care of my own basic needs, much less a dog. I was not intending to become a pet owner in the immediate future, and as a result, I did not have any dog food on hand.

The only thing I had left in my cupboards was Honey Nut Cheerios. Dozer and I shared some of the last Honey Nut Cheerios I had on hand.

I had a serious conversation with my then-girlfriend, now wife, about what my options were regarding the dog and what to do next.

All said and done, we decided to keep the dog. What a great decision that was for both him and us.

To me, having Dozer wander into my life so haphazardly was anything but a chance encounter. I firmly believe the trajectory of this relationship was influenced by a higher power. God knew I needed this dog even if I could not arrive at this conclusion myself. This dog really helped secure my relationship with

Jamie and confirmed my permanent footprint in the state of Tennessee.

Dozer was a very easygoing and welcome addition to our entire family, including my parents and brother's family. Dad used to share his cheddar cheese cubes with him, and Dozer loved Dad for that. My brother would always play aggressively with Dozer, and he became used to that "huge guy," which became an inside joke of its own making.

Dozer grew with us as we developed into who we are today. We all moved together from our apartment to a townhouse. From the townhouse, we moved into our first and current home. Dozer was with us as we went from dating to engaged and from engaged to married.

Dozer was our first love before we had kids, and our relationship with him is longer than the duration of our marriage. Then one day, we had our first child, Xander. Dozer adapted to the new challenge well, checking on our baby often. He loved our family, and when we became a family of four people with the addition of Brantley, Dozer continued to adapt and did it well. Far better than I could have anticipated. Dozer was very tolerant of the boys, and it's a good thing because children can really test anyone's limits, but especially a pet with ears and a tail.

Today marks thirteen years and two days that Dozer was in our lives. This morning we all realized how heavy and somber this day was going to be, but I only thought I knew. I held Dozer's head and reassured him through tear-filled eyes that it would be okay. I thanked him for being such a great dog and let him know that he was so loved and appreciated.

We prayed over him, thanking God for the kind

Some of Andy L. Vistrand's fondest memories with his dog are of Dozer's love for the snow. The Vistrands' memories with Dozer are priceless.

soul the Lord put in our lives and allowing him to be our family pet. He tucked his head onto my left rib hiding his face almost as if he were hugging me, reassuring me that it was time.

I held his head until he took his final breath.

Since those moments, there has been a tremendous sorrow. My heart has been ripped from my chest. I cannot even begin to tell you how much this dog meant to us. He was such a beautiful soul, and I thank God for every single day that he was with us. He will be so dearly missed.

We love you, Dozer. We are so relieved that you are
no longer in pain, but selfishly, we miss you immensely.
Your absence will be felt for quite some time.
Thank you for everything.

That social media post said it all. It contained every raw
emotion that we experienced with our loving Dozer.

As a family, we were there with him in his final moments.

I held his head, and as he became too tired to stand, I securely
supported his head and upper body as we slowly descended in
a controlled and methodical manner to the tabletop. I held him
and reassured him that it was okay, everything would be alright.
Through tear-filled eyes, I said my goodbyes and thanked him
for all that he had done for us. I held him as he approached and
crossed the rainbow bridge to the loving arms of our father, Jesus.
We were doing the right thing for him, but I was dying inside.

Dozer would surely be missed, more than I was aware.

Dozer taught Andy's sons about life, affection, and responsibility. His passing taught them how to grieve, and how to appreciate our blessings.

CHAPTER 11

"The Lord is close to the brokenhearted;
he rescues those whose spirits are crushed."

Psalm 34:18

The Aftermath

The candle on the receptionist's desk in the vet's office danced delicately. On the side of the candle, it read: *If this candle is lit, then someone is saying goodbye to their beloved pet. Please stay quiet during this very difficult time – The Staff.*

Our entire family was devastated. We were all grieving in our own ways. Thirteen years and two days of cherished memories—plus a bond of friendship stronger than anything built of steel and concrete—had come to a sad end. Our world was crumbling.

We stepped into the lobby while they prepared Dozer for the final viewing. This would be the final time we would see our Dozer.

We stood in the lobby, sobbing, our hearts shattered into splinters. Patrons came and went. All were silent. The looks on their faces reassured us that they likely had been where we were, at some point. I held my family and tried to keep it together for them, but in that moment I felt like I had lost a piece of me.

This probably sounds counterintuitive, but as sad as it was, I would not have changed how any of it transpired. As a family, we prayed over Dozer and thanked God for the amazing dog that he blessed us with, and the life we shared. We loved him with every fiber of our being, and he reciprocated that sentiment tenfold.

Throughout our lives, Dozer and I gave each other what each of us was missing. Our circumstances were like missing puzzle pieces being assembled. Thirteen years and two days came down to this: Saying goodbye to him was one of the absolute hardest things I ever had to do. I am not naïve. I know, like anyone else on earth, that life has a beginning and an end. I always knew that the day would come when I would have to say goodbye, and subconsciously, I knew that day would come sooner than I wanted or expected.

The realization that Dozer would leave us one day was incomprehensible and left us grief-stricken. That dog was so much more than a family pet, he was our best friend, a brother to our children. He was the shepherd of our flock, a protector of our home, lives, and property. He was a cherished member of this family, and equivalent in stature to another human being.

In the days that followed his passing at the veterinarian's office, his remains were gently prepared by Eternity Acres Pet Mortuary in Kentucky. They provided us with several keepsakes, including an ink stamp of his paw print, a heart-shaped cast paw print, a small bottle of his hair, an urn containing his ashes, and a certificate. Some days later, we also received sympathy cards from our vet's office and from the crematorium that cared for Dozer's remains so delicately.

We have the keepsakes on display on a shelf in the living room of our home, accompanied by a picture of our first family pet. The legend, Dozer, the vagrant puppy, who set the bar so high for future canines of Vistrand lineage. To see his picture every day reminds me of how lucky we were to have been blessed with a dog like Dozer, because he truly was one of a kind.

CHAPTER 12

"God's voice thunders in marvelous ways;
he does great things beyond our understanding."

Job 37:5

The Unexplainable

Divine intervention is a drastic deviation in the face of seemingly impossible odds. It is unforgettable because it occurs where no hope is present, according to motivational speaker and writer Michael Adarkwah.[10]

I was truly in the darkest hours of my adult life. I was a recently separated military combat veteran, struggling to reinvent myself in the civilian sector. Adding insult to injury, I had relocated eight hundred miles from everything I knew, including the one place I called home for eighteen years of my early life.

I had no friends, knew very little of my surroundings, and was in my first real civilian job, where the enormity of responsibilities were congruent to the earnings. It was a good job, a demanding job, a dangerous job, and a job that was very similar to the military, due to the long periods of time away from home.

The pressure to succeed post-military was always intense.

Even though it was not intended to be this way, I always felt as though the military expected people who separated to fail and come crawling back to them because on the inside, the veteran had purpose and hope. On the outside, all bets were off, and success rested heavily on the shoulders of those hardened warriors who had experienced enough real life to get themselves into trouble but afforded them few resources to rescue them should they get in over their heads.

This kind of stigma was not helpful in most cases, but in this case, it made me rebellious, almost to a fault. That rebellious side of me may have kept me in Tennessee long enough to allow God to work his magic, and if that was the case, I am thankful for it. I remember considering my options. To this day, I have the list of pros and cons that I had drafted considering my options to stay and endure or leave and admit defeat.

Our God is an awesome God. Adarkwah points out that God's divine intervention can see you through anything. It did for me: His involvement changed my status from victim to victor. He stepped in when I was at my weakest and ready to step out. God's divine intervention found me, and not a moment too soon.[11]

For the record, I am glad that I endured. The payoff? My own family was the real reward here. It is a little hard at times to wrap my head around it. To look back at how our paths crossed, I acknowledge it was nothing short of a miracle how it all worked out. I am a firm believer in the fact that God had some kind of divine intervention in the trajectory of our lives. There is absolutely no way our introduction was just a happenstance.

If any one of the many circumstances that happened in the first hours or days before we met had taken an alternative route, my whole life may not have been what it is right now. Jamie might not have been my wife; I might not have my children, Xander and Brantley. I might not even be living in the state of Tennessee.

Lance Cpl. Andy L. Vistrand, right, inspects an aircraft with other members of his crew. After a military career, veterans often feel pressure to succeed. Vistrand sometimes felt as though the military expected people who separated to come back because the military offered a sense of purpose some veterans struggle to find on the outside.

Dozer entering my life when he did strengthened and confirmed my permanent establishment in Tennessee.

To ponder on that is deep. Who knew that something as simple as encountering and adopting a pet would literally be the end of all consideration of defeat? Even after Dozer and I met, life was not easy, but it was bearable. I owe Dozer a great debt of gratitude for the role he played in making me whole again and helping me regain control of a rogue situation from which it seemed there was no recovery. I know he saved my life. He was a real guardian angel sent to me in a time of tremendous need.

Likewise, Dozer was in need, perhaps as badly as I was or more so. He required food, water, shelter, companionship, and care, especially in that young stage of life. Who knows what his living

Andy L. Vistrand came along when this abandoned dog needed him most. However, the truth of their meeting is deeper and more profound than a rescued dog, because Dozer came along just when Andy needed him most.

conditions or his treatment were prior to having been dumped out in our apartment complex.

Having been abandoned some time during that bitterly cold week, Dozer might not have survived if it had not been for our meeting that night.

God had a hand in ensuring we came together in one of the most extraordinary and mutually beneficial interventions of a lifetime. I am still astounded by the odds of this meeting; it was too tall an order to just be luck. The odds are stacked heavily against any solution of this magnitude for two living beings. I thank God for his involvement in my life that day and in the life of my Dozer.

Andy L. Vistrand holds a framed paw print from Dozer, the sidekick and best friend who found Andy just when the Marine veteran needed him most. Dozer was part of Andy's family for many years.

CHAPTER 13

*"His divine power has given us everything we need for a godly life
through our knowledge of him
who called us by his own glory and goodness."*

2 Peter 1:3

The Conclusion

When I began my journey, I thought I had things figured out, but when I encountered an unforeseen circumstance, this really stunted my personal and professional growth. It made me question my decision and challenge my position on where I was in life and if I had made the right call. I was already an introvert, but the fallout made me become even more reclusive. I had never been in such a position. What I thought was a situation under control was an illusion. I was running on fumes; in a matter of time, I'd fail and run out of financial aid and confidence to carry on.

At the time, I was unaware what an honor it was to have such a loyal companion in Dozer. He was kind, caring, compassionate, and no matter how bad my day was, he was always there for me in a special way with the wag of a tail. I am my own worst critic, and

Dozer was a very pleasant distraction from the failure over which I was harshly reprimanding myself.

Although he never received any formal training to be a therapy dog, that is what Dozer became for me.

The word in this case is *resilience*. Resilience means adapting to the surprises life throws at us, the unpredictable changes and complications. Mayo Clinic outlines a number of ways to build resilience when faced with adversity: connecting with family and friends, making every day meaningful, learning from experience, remaining hopeful, taking care of yourself, and being proactive.[12]

Now, this all sounds great, but following through may not be as easy or as effective. When you've tried all those suggestions and haven't overcome challenges, where do you turn?

Therapy dogs could be one solution.

Dogs can be trained to help with a multitude of conditions, according to Northwest Battle Buddies. NWBB is a charitable organization that gifts trained service dogs to veterans, helping them regain their independence.

Therapy dogs trained to help veterans cope with the debilitating symptoms of post-traumatic stress disorder wake their veteran from nightmares; anticipate, alert, and intervene in panic attacks; divert attention from flashbacks; apprise on adrenaline; provide a social barrier in public; furnish security and safety; and perform specific calming remedies such as pressure therapy.[13]

Veterans have seen significant impact in their health as a result of a dog. Most notably, similar to the hospital patients discussed earlier, veterans have reduced prescribed medications as a result of interaction with a therapy dog. With their animal's help, veterans reintegrate into society and overcome social barriers that arise because of PTSD. They often become strong advocates of dogs. So it is really a mutually beneficial relationship.[14]

"Veterans become more engaged with their families. With the help of their service dog, veterans regain control of their lives.

Jamie and Andy L. Vistrand walk with Dozer. Andy marvels at the impact the dog had on his life. Caring for the puppy brought Andy and Jamie closer together. Rescuing the dog gave this Marine veteran a new purpose and a new best friend; it helped him focus on something outside himself during a dark time of his life. Andy didn't realize it right away, but this was a rescue that worked both ways. In so many ways, it was the dog who rescued *him*.

When our veterans are engaged at home, the entire family unit thrives. In many ways, the true impact that a service dog has on the life of a veteran, the veteran's family and community, is immeasurable," Northwest Battle Buddies says on its website.[15]

Owning a dog is not all bliss. There are demands that you cannot overlook when taking responsibility for another life. It's not only the obvious chores: feeding and watering. You need to be observant of flea and tick seasons to make sure the dog is treated to avoid parasitic infestation. You also need to be aware of the dangers of heartworms and treat your dog. If heartworms are left untreated, they can be fatal.

Your dog needs your attention; you need to love and care for it. Dogs need to be bathed, have their nails trimmed, and their coats brushed periodically. Play is also a must; most dogs are energetic. They need, in fact, crave, that interaction with their person.

Without a doubt, some of the tougher responsibilities include being the voice of reason and doing what is right and humane for the dog in its final days or hours, no matter how hard it is for you. This includes, but is not limited to, making the decision to humanely euthanize the dog when the time has come. It is not easy. Nothing about that decision is simple, but if you love your dog and respect the animal enough, you will do what is best for him or her and not for yourself in those final moments of life. Selfishly, no one wants to say goodbye to their lifelong friend. We human beings owe it to our dogs to be strong for them, and when it's time, be ready to make the call.

If there is anything I can say that we as family took away from having to make that call with Dozer, it's this. The boys learned a valuable lesson in life that day. They learned that making tough decisions is a part of life.

Life doesn't go on forever. Animals, no matter how insignificant some people may think they are, play an integral role in our lives. The boys learned the sting of loss and how to grieve. They learned

Dozer rolls over for a belly rub from Xander Vistrand. Being a pet owner brings with it a slew of responsibilities beyond feeding and bathing, but it can be so very rewarding for those who commit to it. Pets need your company, attention, and love, but they will return it tenfold. Dozer taught Andy L. Vistrand's sons about more than belly rubs and ear scratches. The boys learned about life, affection, and responsibility.

to respect life and its many challenges, including death. They also learned the proper way to care for and love an animal.

I have no doubt that my kids can be respectful pet owners one day based on the example that has been set for them. They learned to physically be with Dozer in his final moments. Dogs spend a lifetime sharing their lives with and being loyal to their owners. It is imperative that we be with them in their final moments of life.

If you ever do find yourself in a position where you have to make the call to put your dog to sleep, please have the strength and mental stamina to be there in his or her final moments. They have given you and your family so much. Why not do what you can to repay some of that debt? Be there and escort your beloved dog to the rainbow bridge.

It is cowardly to leave your pet unattended to be euthanized; that is disgusting. They share every moment with us in our lives; the least we can do is be there with them at the end. We do it for our beloved human family members, so why not for our furry family members as well? To me, there is no difference.

I have heard that the reason that dogs age so quickly is because human beings do not deserve dogs. Columnist Rex Huppke of Chicago wrote an article titled "We don't deserve dogs, yet they accept and adore us." The article really helped frame the family dog that was Huppke's writing companion. He makes some very bold statements; even the good people he knows are plagued with more flaws than dogs. People love but with boundaries and conditions, and dogs say much more with a wag of a tail than most people do talking.[16]

Judging by the way Dozer was abandoned at my apartment complex, I can say I agree with that statement. How can anyone just dump an animal out to fend for itself? Some of the very best pets I have owned, including Dozer, have been abandoned by a human being. That is amazing and disgusting. I find it inexplicable how an animal can ever be loyal to another human being after having been

Dozer wasn't always a good boy—like when he chewed the furniture or had a run-in with a skunk—but the benefits of loving him were far beyond good. Dozer improved Andy L. Vistrand's life in too many ways to count.

abandoned. Yet, I rejoice that dogs are forgiving, so that I can do my best to show them what love is and give them the life that they deserve. While I do not condone abandonment or cruelty, I can also say that it is because of those circumstances that I got my chance with Dozer. That person's cruelty and loss became my gain.

Dog ownership provides a vast number of benefits. The relationship between man and dog is one that has been evolving for thousands of years. What have we learned from interaction with these animals? Dogs give so much more than companionship. Owning a dog has been proven to exponentially improve one's mood, health, and energy. Many college campuses and hospitals use dogs to benefit students and patients. Owning a dog can prevent cardiovascular ailments. Dog ownership has even been linked to longer life expectancy for those who have previously suffered from a major cardiac event.

Dogs help us interact with one another, sparking conversation wherever we may go. Dogs have been proven to increase physical interaction with individuals suffering from intellectual disabilities. And, of course, they reduce loneliness. They increase our potential for courtship by merely appearing in photos with us.

People feel strongly about their dogs. The benefits of dog ownership far outweigh the costs. I found this out firsthand with the dog that my family came to know and love as our Dozer. His ability to brighten the darkness with just a simple wag of his tail or nudge from his wet nose was all I needed to become healed in the deepest parts of my soul. Sharing this life with him was not only an honor, it was one of my most rewarding experiences. He brought the best out of me and those around him.

We have been blessed to have dogs. For that, I am so thankful.

Dozer rescued me from darkness.

In doing so, he brightened thirteen years and two days of my life and prevented the unthinkable.

One of the first photos of Dozer shows off the new red collar that welcomed him to the household and made him an official Vistrand family dog.

Notes

1.   Leanne Lewis Newman, "Faith, Spirituality, and Religion: A Model for Understanding the Differences," *The College of Student Affairs Journal* (2004), https://files.eric.ed.gov

2.   Livingston, Cydney, "Man's Best Friend, Our Relationship to Dogs," *Duke Research Blog* (2020), https://researchblog.duke.edu/

3.   Livingston, "Man's Best Friend."

4.   Livingston, "Man's Best Friend."

5.   Livingston, "Man's Best Friend."

6.   Bureau of Labor Statistics, "The Recession of 2007-2009," *Bureau of Labor Statistics* website (February 2012), https://www.bls.gov/spotlight/2012/recession/

7.   Joseph Stromberg. "New Study Shows That Dogs Use Color Vision After All," *Smithsonian Magazine* (2013), https://www.smithsonianmag.com

8.   "Black Mouth Cur," *Wikipedia* (2023), https://en.wikipedia.org/wiki/Black_Mouth_Cur

9.   *Wikipedia*, "Black Mouth Cur."

10. Michael A. Adarkwah, "Divine Intervention," *White Throne Ministries* (2023), https://whitethroneministries.org/blogs/devotions/divine-intervention

11. Adarkwah, "Divine Intervention."

12. Mayo Clinic Staff, "Resilience: Build skills to endure hardship," *Mayo Foundation for Medical Education and Research* (2023), https://www.mayoclinic.org/tests-procedures/resilience-training/in-depth/resilience/art-20046311

13. Northwest Battle Buddies, "Service Dogs: How It Works," *Northwest Battle Buddies* (2023), https://northwestbattlebuddies.org/veterans/service-dogs

14. Northwest Battle Buddies, "Service Dogs."

15. Northwest Battle Buddies, "Service Dogs."

16. Rex Huppke, "We don't deserve dogs, yet they accept and adore us," *Idaho Mountain Express* (2020), https://www.mtexpress.com/

ANDY L. VISTRAND

Andy L. Vistrand was born in Niobe, New York. He is an animal lover who grew up with pets, more specifically, English Bulldogs. He attended Panama Central School and graduated in 2003 with a Regents High School Diploma. He enlisted in the Marines after high school and served his country for five years.

Vistrand is an honorably discharged Marine combat veteran and former law enforcement officer. His active-duty service to the United States military included deployments to Iraq on three occasions. Vistrand served as a UH-1N Huey Helicopter crew chief, logging nearly one thousand hours in flight time. Over six hundred hours of that time is red hours, or combat flight time. Rising to the rank of corporal, he earned the distinction of weapons and tactics instructor for all squadron purposes and missions.

Vistrand served for five years as a law enforcement officer, serving in two West Tennessee municipalities. He earned notable distinction as a law enforcement professional, having become certified in advance roadside impaired driving enforcement.

Vistrand earned his bachelor of science degree with honors in business management from Bethel University.

A family man dedicated to community service, Vistrand is an active member serving in an officer capacity in the Jackson, Tennessee, Marine Corps League Detachment. There, he leads the Toys for Tots campaign in his home county, among other responsibilities.

Milton Keynes UK
Ingram Content Group UK Ltd.
UKHW020317211123
432926UK00002B/55